PARENTS' PERCEPTIONS OF THEIR ADOLESCENTS' ATTITUDES TOWARDS SUBSTANCE USE
BY ETHNIC DIFFERENCES

Dr. Vernita Black

authorHOUSE®

AuthorHouse™
1663 Liberty Drive
Bloomington, IN 47403
www.authorhouse.com
Phone: 1 (800) 839-8640

© 2016 Dr. Vernita Black. All rights reserved.

No part of this book may be reproduced, stored in a retrieval system, or transmitted by any means without the written permission of the author.

Published by AuthorHouse 10/14/2016

ISBN: 978-1-5246-1225-2 (sc)
ISBN: 978-1-5246-1224-5 (e)

Library of Congress Control Number: 2016908977

Print information available on the last page.

Any people depicted in stock imagery provided by Thinkstock are models, and such images are being used for illustrative purposes only. Certain stock imagery © Thinkstock.

This book is printed on acid-free paper.

Because of the dynamic nature of the Internet, any web addresses or links contained in this book may have changed since publication and may no longer be valid. The views expressed in this work are solely those of the author and do not necessarily reflect the views of the publisher, and the publisher hereby disclaims any responsibility for them.

TABLE OF CONTENTS

List of Tables vii

CHAPTER ONE: THE PROBLEM 1
Introduction 1
Problem Background 2
    Teen Illicit Drug Use 3
    Teen Alcohol Use 5
    Adolescents Substance Use by Ethnic Groups 6
    Parent's Perceptions 7
    Adolescent's Attitudes toward Substance Use 9
Purpose of the Study 10
Research Questions 10
Definition of Key Terms 11
Limitations of the Study 12
Significance of the Study 13
Summary 14

CHAPTER TWO: LITERATURE REVIEW 15
Review of Literature 15
Adolescent Attitudes toward Substance Use 15
Adolescents Alcohol and Drug Use among Ethnic Groups ... 16
Parents Perceptions of Adolescents' Attitudes toward Substance Use 20
Parents Perception of Substance Use by Ethnic Backgrounds 21
Summary 23

CHAPTER THREE: METHOD 24
Introduction 24
Research Design 24
Selection of Participants 25
Instrumentation and Data Collection Strategies 25
Procedure 26
Data Analysis 27

Assumptions of this Study 28

CHAPTER FOUR: FINDINGS 29
Restatement of the Purpose 29
Demographics 30
Restatement of Purpose 33
Analysis of Responses to Survey Questions 33
    Research Question 1a 33
    Research Question 1b 34
    Research Question 2 36
    Research Question 3 37
    Research Question 4 39
Summary 40

CHAPTER FIVE: DISCUSSION, RECOMMENDATION AND SUMMARY 41
Discussion of Study and Purpose Justification 41
Interpretation of Data 42
Demographic Profile 43
Discussion of Key Themes 44
Study Limitation 49
Implications 50
Recommendations 51
Recommendations for Future Research 52
Summary 52

REFERENCES 55
APPENDIX A: SURVEY 61
    Appendixes 63

LIST OF TABLES

Table 1 Descriptive Statistics for the Participants' Demographics 31
Table 2 Descriptive Statistics for the Adolescents' Demographics 32
Table 3 Means and Standard Deviations of Parent Perceptions by Ethnicity 34
Table 4 One-way ANOVA on Parent Perceptions by Ethnicity 34
Table 5 Means and Standard Deviations of Parent Perceptions by Ethnicity 35
Table 6 One-way ANOVA on Parent Perceptions by Ethnicity 36
Table 7 Means and Standard Deviations of Parent Perceptions of Peer Drug Modeling by Ethnicity 37
Table 8 One-way ANOVA on Parent Perceptions by Ethnicity 37
Table 9 Means and Standard Deviations of Parent Perceptions of Self-Esteem by Ethnicity 38
Table 10 One-way ANOVA on Parent Perceptions by Ethnicity 39
Table 11 Means and Standard Deviations of Parent Perceptions of Positive Peer Modeling by Ethnicity 40
Table 12 One-way ANOVA on Parent Perceptions by Ethnicity 40
Table 13 Descriptive Statistics for Perceptions of Attitudes towards Substance Use 74
Table 14 Descriptive Statistics for Perceptions of Attitudes towards Substance Use 75
Table 15 Descriptive Statistics for Perceptions of Peer Drug Modeling 76
Table 16 Descriptive Statistics for Perceptions of Self-Esteem 77
Table 17 Descriptive Statistics for Perceptions of Positive Peer Modeling 78

CHAPTER ONE

THE PROBLEM

Introduction

In the last few decades, there has been a huge increase in the number of drug use among our nation's youth. National survey data show that drug use among our Nation's youth is increasing at an alarming rate. Some say we are on the verge of major epidemic. However, 20 years of research have now provided the tools to change current course of events and to reverse the increases in teenage drug use that began in 1992. We know now the causes of drug use and abuse than ever before, and we have learned a great deal about what works and what does not. We are beyond the point where we have to make uninformed choices about what might prevent or reduce teenage drug use (Botvin, 2006).

Alcohol, tobacco and other drug use, misuse and abuse have continued to be a major issue at the National and local level. In 2003, 19.5 million people or 8.2 percent of the population in the United States age 12 or older used illicit drugs (Substance Abuse and Mental Health Services Administration, 2003).

This research compared the attitudes of 7th to 12th graders of differing ethnic backgrounds regarding alcohol and substance use from their parent's perception. The research took place in 2009 school year. This research study utilized survey data to determine parent's perception of their adolescents' attitude toward substance use. Chapter 1 was divided into eight sections as follows: (a) introduction; (b) background of the problems; (c) purpose of the study; (d) research questions; (e) definition of key terms; (f) limitations of study; (g) significance of the study; and (h) overview of the study.

Problem Background

The Adolescent drug use epidemic in the United States dates back over 20 years. Beginning in the 1960's when much of the nation's youth began to use psychoactive drugs such as LSD and PCP, the drug epidemic created public concern as it continued into the 70's. The 1980's showed much of the same with drug use on the rise (Center for Substance Abuse Prevention, 1993).

Considering that alcohol and drug use has created concerns since the early 70's, it is important to present problems associated with children regarding attitudes of alcohol and substance use. Current research, thus far, have primarily focused on alcohol and substance use among children and adults. Although this matter is important, this investigation expands beyond the current substance use by examining parents' perceptions of their adolescent's attitudes toward substance use by ethnic differences. The proposed research study investigated whether differences in parents' perception exist between the varied ethnic groups.

According to the Education Resources Information Center (1983), the problem of drug and alcohol use among young people has caused concern for many years. A survey of students' attitudes concerning drugs and alcohol use was conducted by the classroom publication "Weekly Reader." Students in grades 4 through 12 responded to the poll, and a random sample of 101,000 responses was analyzed.

The results of the poll showed that in grades four and five, children reported that learning about the dangers of drugs and drinking from family, movies and television. Not until grade six did school become the major source of information. As early as grade four, about 25 percent of the students said that children in their age group felt peer pressure to try alcohol or marijuana. By seventh grade, at least half of the respondents felt pressure to experiment with alcohol and marijuana. Although other studies have indicated that drug use among students is not as high as these students believed, the fact that young students think drug use is common in itself cause for concern since many children use drugs to fit in and gain acceptance.

A multitude of research over the past five years has shown both positive and negative relationships regarding substance use among adolescents. Yet, adolescents are still experiencing problems with substance use around the world. In the last few decades, there has been a huge increase in the number of adolescents in various ethnic backgrounds that have experienced issues with substance use.

Drug use among teenagers in the United States is a serious concern. In 2003 more than 7.5 million individuals aged 12 to 17 reported having used an illicit drug at least once in their lifetime (U. S. Department of Justice, 2003).

Overall, the Household Survey found that 15.9 million Americans age 12 and older used an illicit drug in the month immediately prior to the survey interview. This represents an estimated 7.1 percent of the population in 2001, compared to an estimated 6.3 percent the previous year (Substance Abuse Mental Health Service Administration, 2001).

The National Survey on Drug Use (2007) stated that illicit drug use among teens age 12-17 was at a five-year low, according to the largest most comprehensive study of drug use in the United States. Despite these trends, non-medical use of painkillers continues to be an area of concern than any illicit drug.

A study from the Substance Abuse and Mental Health Services Administration (2009), says that prescription painkillers misuse among young adults has increased even as non-medical use by teenagers decreased between 2002 and 2007. Additionally, the study indicated that trends in Non-Medical Use of Prescription Pain Relievers; 2002-2007, found that misuse of prescription painkillers increased from 4.1 percent in 2006 to 4.6 percent in 2007 among young adults.

Teen Illicit Drug Use

Substance use is one of today's most challenging health and social problems. Further, it is more pervasive in the United States than any other industrialized nation. Early involvement with any drug use is a risk factor for later drug use and criminal activity, and the more severe the early involvement, the greater the risk that anti-social behavior will emerge in the future. Early years of alcohol, tobacco, or illicit drugs has been linked clearly to substance abuse (Newcomb & Abbott, 1996).

According to Sloboda & Stephens (2001), a study conducted by the University of Akron Institute for Health and Social Policy, the study indicates that at least half of all adolescents have tried illicit drugs, alcohol, or tobacco by the time they finish high school. The Monitoring the Future Study conducted by the University of Michigan (2000) confirmed this finding.

The Monitoring the Future Study also found that by the time teens reach 12th grade, about one in five seniors gets drunk regularly while slightly less, 31 percent, of 12th graders smoke cigarettes.

In 2000, approximately 52 percent of youths aged 12 to 17 who were daily cigarette smokers, and 66 percent of youths who were heavy drinkers, were also past month users of illicit drugs. Youths who were daily cigarette smokers or heavy drinkers were more likely than either daily smokers or heavy drinkers from older age groups (National Household Survey on Drug Abuse, 2001).

The National Household Survey on Drug Abuse (2003), indicate that some children are already abusing illicit drugs by the age of 12 or 13 which likely means that some may begin even earlier. Early abuse includes such drugs as tobacco, alcohol, inhalants, marijuana, and psycho therapeutic drug.

According to the Substance Abuse and Mental Health Services Administrator's 2006 National Survey on Drug and Health, an estimated 111,774,000 Americans 12 years of age and older had used an illicit drug at least once during their lifetimes.

Illicit drugs pose serious dangers for teens. Illicit drugs use is against the law. More than four in ten adolescents have been offered drugs at some point and about one in four have been offered drugs at school. The most commonly used illicit drug for 12-17-year-old is marijuana. In 2006, almost one third (32%) of 12 graders reported smoking marijuana, while one-quarter (25%) of 10th graders and one-eight (12%) of 8th graders did. But there are also other illicit drugs out there that teens are exposed to. Amphetamines, inhalants, and prescription drugs, are just some examples. Though still too high, research tells us that the trends for some of these drugs are promising (U. S. Department of Health and Human Services (2008).

The latest survey shows that by age 16 substantial majorities of young people believe that marijuana use is common among their peers and that this drug is as easy to obtain as alcohol. Seven out of ten students in grade 11 believed that half or more of their age peers had tried marijuana. Eight out of ten reported that both alcohol and marijuana were easily or fairly easy to obtain (Johnson, Bachman & O'Malley, 1999).

Teen Alcohol Use

Teen use of alcohol has also been tracked. According to the Alcohol Policies Project (2002), approximately 9.7 million people who drink alcohol in the United States are between the ages of 12-20. Of these young drinkers, 18.7 percent are binge drinkers and 6% are heavy drinkers. On an average, young people begin drinking at 13.1 years of age, and by the time they are in high school, 80 percent used alcohol and 6 percent have been drunk (p.5).

Despite two decades of the "war on drugs" in the United States, adolescent substance use remains a major health and safety problem. Many adolescents have tried alcohol as early as eight-grade and by the time they graduate from high school.

According to the Monitoring the Future study, a long-term survey of behaviors, attitudes, and values of American secondary students, and young adults, has been tracking rates of alcohol and other substance use among youth for the past 25 years. The most recent figures of that study indicated that 80 percent of adolescents have consumed alcohol by their senior year in high school, with over one-half having done so by the eight-grade (Johnston, O'Malley & Bachman, 1999).

The Center of Addiction for Substance Abuse (2005), reported that a troubling finding from this year's survey was the increase in the number of teens who report that their peers use illegal drugs. From 2004 to 2005, the percentage of teens who know friend or classmate that has abused prescription drugs jumped 86 percent (from 14 percent to 26 percent). The percentage of teens who know a friend or classmate that has used Ecstasy is up 28 percent (from 18 percent to 28 percent). The percentage of teens who know a friend or classmate that has used illegal drugs such as acid, cocaine or heroin is up 20 percent (from 35 percent to 42 percent).

In the United States, there have been many studies regarding alcohol use among children and adults. Yet, alcohol use is still on the rise around the world. Payne (2002) described alcohol use as the second leading cause of dementia; one simply ages quicker on alcohol. But professionals today are worried about a steady increase in teen alcohol use and abuse and the possible negative health effects.

Adolescents Substance Use by Ethnic Groups

In most parts of the world, adolescents are experiencing illicit drug use. This support may vary among ethnic groups. According to the National survey on Drug Use and Health (2002), the rates of current illicit drug use were highest among American Indians/Alaska Natives (10.1) and persons reporting two or more races (11.4). Rates were 9.7 for blacks, 8.5 percent for whites and 7.2 percents for Hispanics. Asians had the lowest rate at 3.5 percent.

Drug use among ethnic groups, presents information about the nature and extent of drug use and its adverse consequences among four major racial classification used by the U. S. Census Bureau: American Indians/Alaska Natives, Asians/Pacific Islanders, African Americans, and Hispanics (National Institute on Drug Abuse, 2005).

Analysis of 1991-1993 data from the National Household Survey of Drug Abuse (1993), shows that there are disparities in level of illicit drugs, alcohol and tobacco use among the 11 racial/ethnic subgroups that make up the total of the United States. Native American Indians and Alaska Natives) exhibited a higher prevalence of illicit drug use 19.8 percent. Rates of prevalence exhibited by other subgroups are Puerto Ricans (13.3%), African Americans (13.1%), Mexican Americans (12.7%), Caucasians (11.8%), South Cuban Americans (8.2%), Caribbean American (7.6%), Asian/Pacific Islanders (6.5%) and Central Americans (5.7%).

Previous research based on major surveys has focused primarily on differences in substance use prevalence among three major racial/ethnic groups-Hispanics, non-Hispanic Blacks, and non-Hispanic

Whites. More is known about three major racial/ethnic differences among adolescents than among adults in the United States because several major national surveys focus on substance use among adolescent respondents (U. S. Department of Health and Human Services, 2008).

Parent's Perceptions

In terms of measuring parent's perception of their children's alcohol and drug use, previous research has focused on a comparative analysis of parental perception and reported youth substance use (Freidman & Utada, 1990, Cohen 1995, Donnell, 1998 Bierut & Fisher, 2006). These research finding suggest that in general that parental awareness of the extent of substance use amongst their children is low. In relation to such estimation within the treatment sector, Friedman and Utada (1990) found that mothers reported low estimation of their children's substance use and a greater perception of the problem associated with the substance.

According to Donnermeyer (2000), there are few studies of parents' views about alcohol and substance use prevention in general, or specific prevention education activities. Yet, their perceptions are important because families are a primary socialization source, and because parents' opinion can either reinforce or countermand the message of alcohol and substance use among adolescents.

Parents seem to be more informed today about alcohol and drug use than ten years ago. Teachers, principals and parents are providing information to their children regarding alcohol and drug use.

Donnermeyer (2000) also stated that parents' opinion contributes to community norms about substance use and community support for prevention education. Parents are voters and tax payers and their opinions influence the decisions of the police, school officials, and political leaders about the adoption and continuation of prevention education efforts of alcohol and substance use. Thompson and Walters (2003) found that fewer teens are using drugs because of the deliberate and serious messages they have received about the dangers of drug from their parents, leaders and prevention efforts.

According to the United States Department of Health and Human Services (2004), a child is an individual with hopes, fears, likes, dislikes, and special talents. The more you know about your child, the easier it will be to guide him/her toward more positive activities and friendships. As a result, the child will be less likely to experiment with alcohol tobacco or illegal drugs (U. S. Department of Health and Human Service, 2004).

Parent's perceptions of their children's attitude of alcohol and substance use may present pertinent information not necessarily revealed by children. Therefore, it is important to assess parent's perception to help determine if attitudes regarding alcohol and substance use are changing among the differing ethnic backgrounds of adolescents.

According to the National Survey of American Attitudes on Substance Abuse (2002), many parents think they have little power over their teens' substance use and a disturbing number view drugs in schools as a fact of life they are powerless to stop. How parents act, how much pressure they put on school administrators to get drugs out of their teens' schools, their attitudes about drugs, and how engaged they are in their children's lives will have enormous influence over their teen's substance use. Parent Power is the most underutilized weapon in efforts to curb teen substance use. Contrary to popular beliefs, most parents are aware of and can accurately evaluate the extent of their teenager's drinking, cigarette smoking, marijuana use and overall substance abuse. Parents who underestimate their teen's substance use usually do so because they have personal substance abuse issues themselves (Gans, 2007).

Recent studies indicate that parents have their own issues with substance use, which in most cases contributes to their children's problems. According to a study conducted by the Journal of Child and Adolescent Substance Abuse (2007), parents have their own problems with substance use. Of the parents in the study who under reported their teen's substance abuse, the study found that the parent had personal problems such as stress or depression, they intended to drink frequently, and the parent did less monitoring of after-school activities.

Adolescent's Attitudes toward Substance Use

According to the Eric Digest (2000), the problems of drug and alcohol use among young people has caused concern for many years. A survey of students' attitudes concerning drugs and alcohol use was conducted by the classroom publication "Weekly Reader."

The Weekly Reader also stated that although other studies have indicated that drug use among students is not as high as these students believed, the fact that young students think drug use is common is in itself cause for concern since many children use drugs to fit in and gain acceptance by their peers.

Attitudes toward substance use among adolescents in some cases are viewed as negative and detrimental to health and social situations if used in excess. According to the Journal of Child and Family Studies (2004), most children believed that alcohol use can lead to accidents, that drinking has negative social consequences, and that alcohol use hurts only if done to excess. Indications are that young children generally have negative attitudes regarding alcohol use and that public and family alcohol education effort need to be more specific about deleterious effects of even low levels of alcohol use in the young.

American teens are adopting an increasingly anti-marijuana attitude, according to new findings from the 2003 Teens Partnership Attitude Tracking Study (PATS), release by the Partnership for a Drug-Free America. Researchers suggest the figures show that teens are becoming increasingly aware of the risks of marijuana and are less likely to start using the drug.

Purpose of the Study

The purpose of this quantitative research study was to examine the perceptions of parents regarding adolescents' attitude toward substance use. Specifically, the study compared parents' perceptions of their adolescents' attitudes with regard to differing ethnic backgrounds.

Additionally, the purpose of the current study was to explore and solicit feedback from parents, specifically parents/guardians of adolescents ages 12-17. The study attempted to determine if there were ethnic differences in attitudes toward substance use among adolescents.

Parents play a vital role in their adolescents' attitudes toward substance use. Parents are perceived as most approachable, knowledgeable and more aware of their children's attitudes and behaviors toward substance use. Also, parents contribute to an enormous part of their teens' decision-making process in various aspects of their lives. The examination of parents' perspective of students' attitude regarding alcohol and substance use assisted the researcher in determining if parent's perception can help children resist alcohol and substance use. The researchers' hope from this study was that parents can be more aware of their teen's attitudes toward substance use.

Research Questions

Quantitative research design was used to determine aggregate differences between groups or classes of subjects. Emphasis is placed on precise measurement and controlling for extraneous source of error (Rudestam & Newton, 2007).

For the current study, this researcher wished to learn about the differing ethnic backgrounds of adolescents' attitudes toward substance use. The researcher was particularly interested in finding out the answers to the following key questions.

1. Is there a statistically significant difference between the ethnic groups (African American vs. Caucasian vs. Hispanic vs. Other/Mixed Ethnic Groups) on the parents' perceptions of their adolescents' attitudes towards substance use?

2. Is there a statistically significant difference between the ethnic groups (African American vs. Caucasian vs. Hispanic vs. Other/Mixed Ethnic Groups) on the parent's perceptions of their adolescents' attitude towards substance use of peer drug modeling?

3. Is there a statistically significant difference between the ethnic groups (African American vs. Caucasian vs. Hispanic vs.

Other/Mixed Ethnic Groups) on the parents' perceptions of their adolescents' attitude towards substance use of self-esteem?

4. Is there a statistically significant difference between the ethnic groups (African American vs. Caucasian vs. Hispanic vs. Other/Mixed Ethnic Groups) on the parents' perceptions of their adolescents' attitudes towards positive peer modeling?

Definition of Key Terms

For the purposes of this study, the following operational definitions are used:

Abuse. Use of a drug for a purpose other than a therapeutic one; be addicted to a substance.

Adolescent. The period of life from puberty to maturity, that terminates legally at the age of majority. A stage of development (as of a language or culture) prior to maturity.

Alcohol. Colorless volatile flammable liquid, forming the intoxicating element in wine, beer, liquid, etc. Alcohol is also used as a solvent, as fuel etc.

Alcohol abuse. As described in the DSM-IV, is a psychiatric diagnosis describing the recurring use of alcoholic beverages despite negative consequences. It is differentiated from alcohol dependence by the lack of symptoms such as tolerance and withdrawal. Alcohol abuse is sometimes referred to by the less specific term alcoholism.

However, many definitions of alcoholism exist, and only some are compatible with alcohol abuse.

Attitude. An attitude is a hypothetical construct that represents an individual's degree of like or dislikes for an item. Attitudes are generally positive or negative views of a person, place or thing or event.

Drugs. Drugs are substances intended for use in the diagnosis, cure, mitigation, treatment or prevention of disease. Drugs are also illicit substances that cause addiction, habituation or a marked changed in consciousness.

Drug Use. Drug Use is the use of drugs for psychotropic rather than medical purposes. Among the most common psychotropic drugs are opiates (opium, morphine, heroin, hallucinogens (LSD, psilocybin and barbiturates).

Ethnic. Having a common or national or cultural tradition.

Ethnicity. The terms "ethnicity" and ethnic group are derived from the Greek word ethnos, normally translated as "nation". The modern usage of "ethnic group", however, reflects the different kinds of encounters industrialized states have had with subordinate groups, such as immigrants and colonized subjects; "ethnic group" came to stand in opposition to "nation", to refer to people with distinct cultural identities who, through migration or conquest, had become subject to a foreign state.

Perceptions. In psychology and cognitive sciences, perception is the process of acquiring interpreting, soliciting, and organizing sensory information.

Minority. Relatively small groups of people differing from others in race.

Substance Use. Something (as drugs or alcoholic beverage) deemed harmful and usually subject to legal restrictions. Physical material from which something is made or that has discrete existence.

Limitations of the Study

The overall parameters of the research included statements of limitations.

There were four limitations in this study. They included using a web-based survey to measure parents' perception of adolescents attitudes toward alcohol and substance use this may compromise the validity and reliability of the study.

Another limitation was that the sample was limited to parent's perception of adolescents' attitudes of alcohol and substance use by differing ethnic groups. This may mean that only those parents or guardians who were involved in their teens' lives regarding alcohol and substance use took part in the study. Furthermore, the sample was limited to parent's perceptions of students in 7th-12th grade. Finally, the study subjects were limited to persons who agreed to participate in a web-based study. The data for this study was gathered from participants who had access to a computer. Also, the study required that the participant had a basic understanding of the computer's operation.

Significance of the Study

Research over the past five years in substance use has supported the concept of attitudes of adolescents toward alcohol and substance use. The design and structure of substance use, however, has varied. No one research has looked the same and no one research has worked the same. Despite the inconsistencies of research, organizations and agencies continue to pour millions of dollars in support of adolescents regarding substance use with the hopes of such outcomes as improved student attitudes toward substance use from a parents' perception.

Past studies on alcohol and substance use among adolescents that have included parent's perceptions have found that, often times, parents are unaware and are blind to their children's involvement regarding substance use. Evidence showed that parents are sometimes unaware of their teens' involvement with illicit drugs. For instance, two separate surveys of parents of teenage children found that parents were much likely to believe that their children's friends drink and drive than they were to believe that their own children did.

According to the U.S. Department of Health and Human Services (2004), several recent surveys suggest that parent perceptions of youth drinking are skewed toward underestimating the amount and frequency of use. For example, in one survey, 31 percent of youth who said they had been drunk in the past year were said by their parents to be nondrinkers, and 27 percent of those who said they had 5 or more drinks in the past month were said by their parents to be non drinkers.

The National Center on Addiction and Substance Abuse (2006) found that 80 percent of parents believe that neither alcohol nor marijuana is usually available at parties their teens attend. But 50 percent of teen partygoers attend parties where alcohol, drugs or both are available.

According to the National Analytic Summary (2002), substance use is by no means limited to specific racial or ethnic populations. There is, however, increasing concern about substance use and abuse patterns among racial and ethnic minorities.

It was hoped that this study would shed some light on parents' perception on adolescents' attitude toward substance use. This researcher hoped that information gathered through the current study provided some insight of alcohol and substance use among adolescents.

This researcher was especially interested in looking at the ethnic differences of adolescent's attitudes toward alcohol and substance use. It was hoped that information obtained through this study added to the knowledge base of this area of practice in the drug and alcohol counseling field and helped counselors, parents, and students to improve their knowledge and awareness regarding substance use.

Summary

The attitude of adolescents toward alcohol and substance use and more specifically, among ethnic differences is currently on the rise in the United States. This chapter gave a brief introduction into the study topic and identified areas that required further exploration. The next chapter delves into a depth look at existing literature and research that explored relevant theory and research on alcohol and substance use and more specifically, parent's perceptions of their teens' attitudes toward substance use by differing ethnic background.

CHAPTER TWO

LITERATURE REVIEW

Review of Literature

In the preceding chapter, parents' perception of their children attitudes toward substance use was examined including differing ethnic backgrounds. This chapter reviewed the literature about attitudes of adolescents toward alcohol and substance use from a parent's perception among various ethnic backgrounds. The literature covered alcohol and substance use among White, African American, Asian, Hispanics and other mixed ethnic groups of parents' perception of teens' attitudes toward alcohol and substance use.

Studies on attitudes toward substance use of various adolescents' ethnic groups were more prevalent in the early 1980's and 1990's and because much of the literature is outdated it may not accurately reflect current situations. Hence, wherever available, recent research was selected for review of literature for this study, although a few of the older studies was included. This review proceeded first with a discussion of attitudes of adolescents toward substance use, then within the views of parents' perceptions among adolescent's ethnic groups.

Adolescent Attitudes toward Substance Use

Ross (1991) conducted a research on alcohol and other drug attitudes and use among suburban fifth and sixth-grade students. Despite the fact that this study is almost 17 years old, its finding was too interesting to exclude. Ross surveyed fifth and sixth grade students (N=1,395) from ten K-6 schools in one suburban school district in the Midwest. The Primary Prevention Awareness, Attitudes and Usage Scales Form 9a

(PPAAUS) was used. Gender information particularly with respect to the use of alcohol and cigarettes of boys and girls was also gathered.

A statistical analysis was done and the researcher found that students who report they have used any alcohol numbered 42 percent; intent to use numbered 68 percent. Use and intent to use "hard" drugs were less than 4 percent and 11 percent, respectively. Sixth grade boys reported highest use of alcohol and cigarettes; sixth grade girls four times higher use of cigarettes than fifth grade girls. Furthermore, within group comparison the study shows a significant relationship to use alcohol and cigarettes among gender and grade levels.

Ross (1991) conclusions were drawn from the findings that described developmental differences by gender and grade level. Recommendations were made for K-12 comprehensive prevention programs and for further research.

Another study conducted by The Partnership for a Drug-free America (1999) explored Teens Attitudes toward Drug Improvement. Teens between the ages of 13 to 18 living throughout the United States (N=6,529) were surveyed. The study statistical measures indicate that teenagers are disassociating drugs from critically important badges of teen identity.

The study also found that fewer teens believe that "most people will try marijuana sometimes"—support from this statement declined to 35 percent in 1999, from 40 percent in 1998 and 41 percent in 1997.

Adolescents Alcohol and Drug Use among Ethnic Groups

A Study by Warheit et., al (1996) surveyed minority adolescents regarding illicit drug use among diverse sample of non-Hispanic White, African American, Cuban, and Puerto Rican adolescent's boys. The survey instrument utilized a Likert scale type set of responses and contained questions about alcohol and drug use measures. Subject selection was random as various adolescents of differing ethnic groups were surveyed (N=5,370), of which (N=3,403) were Hispanics.

The results of Warheit (1996) study discussed here are only those related to substance use of multi-ethnic groups among adolescent's boys. The researchers found that substance use among the various groups revealed that although the differences were not significant in all instances both non-Hispanic Whites and Hispanic origin adolescents had higher rates of substance use than African-American. By contrast, few significant differences were found between non-Hispanic Whites and their Hispanic peers (p.11).

When surveyed about substance use among African-American, the researcher found that African-American were less likely than their non-Hispanic counterparts to engage in heavy use of alcohol.

Warheit, et. al (1996) reported that African-Americans viewed alcohol use as being more detrimental to their health than non-Hispanic White (NHW) and that alcohol should be avoided because it is addictive. African-Americans also reported greater concern than NHW about parental disapproval. To date, little research has been reported on the factors underlying the differences in substance use between African-American adolescents and others. It is an area that needs additional, theory driven, hypothesis testing research (p.12).

The other findings of interest here is that when compared to various Hispanics subgroups, there were few significant differences in substance use. The researchers were unclear as to whether this finding reflected differences among Hispanics substance use or other differences. Warheit, et.al (1996) hypothesized that when differences were found they were probably more related to levels of acculturation resulting from length of time in the United States than to nativity. However, the results are not easy to interpret. On the one hand, this hypothesis finds support in the data that showed that although the differences were not always significant, there was a general linear trend between length of time in the United States and increased substance use rates for all four groups (p.12).

As Warheit et. al. (1996) also noted:

> Puerto Rico has common wealth status with the United States. They are included in the analyses as Hispanic under the supposition that their cultural heritage and language use, especially among the foreign born, are sufficiently different from those of non-Hispanic

background United States born adolescents to warrant Cross-group comparisons. An adolescent was placed in a particular subgroup on the basis of his country of birth and/or the birth place of his parents. As noted, about one-half the Hispanic students in the sample were foreign born. The percentage of foreign born for the four groups was: Cubans, 33 percent; Nicaraguans, 92 percent; Colombians, 69 percent; and Puerto Ricans, 81 percent. The average length of time in the United States varied for the four groups (p.18).

The study findings presented have both scientific and programmatic relevance. They confirm and extend the research of others who have studied multi-ethnic samples of adolescents in substance use. The information presented also has important implications for those engaged in planning drug prevention programs aimed at adolescents (p.13).

Another study conducted by the National Survey on Drug Use and Health (2005) reported that research comparing the extent of substance use among Hispanic youths with use among non-Hispanic youths has found mixed results. Hispanic youths aged 12 to 17 were less likely to report past month alcohol use and past month marijuana use than non-Hispanic youths.

In 2002 and 2003, 10.8 percent of Hispanic youths reported illicit drug use in the past month compared with 11.6 of non-Hispanic youths. Hispanic youths were likely to have used marijuana in the past month (6.8 percent than non-Hispanic youths (8.3) (NSDUH, 2005).

Research studies show that attitudes towards alcohol and drug use differ among adolescents according to age, grade and ethnic backgrounds. According NHSDA (2003), examination of ethnic variation in Monitoring the Future (MTF) estimates for 2000, tend to indicate that Hispanic 8th graders are more likely to have started using marijuana, inhalants, LSD, other hallucinogens, and cocaine than 8th grade non-Hispanics, Whites or Blacks. Among 12th graders, Hispanic teens are more likely to have started to use marijuana and cocaine, but not inhalants, LSD, or other hallucinogens (p.62).

The final study found which explored adolescents' attitudes regarding substance use by differing ethnic groups was conducted by Delaney (2002) in a Partnership Attitude Tracking Study (PATS). This study surveyed teens in grades 7-12 and parents with respects to their attitudes about illegal drugs. The data in the report were collected from April through June 2002.

The subject selection was conducted in homes and schools, with selected data using self-report surveys. The author administered the survey instrument to three classes of adolescents' minority groups. The three classes in the study were whites, Hispanic and African Americans teens.

Delaney (2002) was primarily interested in the attitudes or changes in inhalant abuse among white teens and risk of heroin use among African Americans and Hispanics. Her survey tapped into these changes as well as general attitudes of toward illegal drugs among adolescents.

The PATS (2002) study explored various points which are relevant to this research study. The study states that according to leading researchers, there are very interesting differences in adolescent drug use that are found among the three largest ethnic groups-Whites, African American, and Hispanics. The PATS (2002) survey results indicate that after a decade of rising adolescent drug use, anti-drug attitudes are strengthening and teen drug use is declining. African American teens are leading the decrease in teen use of marijuana. They also led the increase in teen use of marijuana in the early 1990s. The lower drug use among African American teens is consistent with leading research showing that African America youth have substantially lower rates of use of most licit and illicit drugs than do Whites or Hispanics.

This finding is not surprising given that, at the time of the 1990 study, labeling theory was relatively new and ideas about marijuana use may not have been thoroughly researched or understood. Delaney (2000) found that, during the 1990's marijuana use significantly increased among African American teens and by 1999 trial of marijuana was significantly higher than White teens and equal to Hispanic teens.

However, since 1999, trial of marijuana significantly decreased among African American teen (47 percent lifetime trial in 1999 to 40 percent in 2002). At the same time, trial of marijuana among Whites

(39 percent in 1999 to 40 percent in 2002) and Hispanics (45 percent in 1999 and 2002) held steady. Of the respondent groups, African American teens had a higher risk of marijuana than Hispanics and African American had a greater risk of marijuana than do Whites teens.

When first surveyed, there were differences in ethnic groups regarding substance use in 2002. Delaney (2002) indicated that there were positive changes in 2002 among all three groups in terms of perceived aspiration risks versus 2001. Compared to 2001 there were no significant differences in general attitudes toward drugs among Whites, African Americans, or Hispanics teens.

Parents Perceptions of Adolescents' Attitudes toward Substance Use

Through the Partnership for a Drug-Free America, Pasierb (2004), conducted the Partnership Attitude Tracking Study (PATS) comparing parental perception of risk of substance from 1988-2004. He found that compared to parents in 1998, those in 2004 were significantly less likely to see great risks for their teens in using marijuana regularly, trying cocaine once or twice, and using cocaine regularly. Additionally, the study indicated that today's parents are significantly less likely than those in 1998 to perceive that their teens sees specific risks in marijuana use—going on to harder drugs, becoming a loser, acting stupidly and foolishly, getting hooked, doing worse at school, work or sports, messing up their lives, or upsetting their parents.

Parents seem to be more informed today about alcohol and drug abuse than ten years ago. Teachers, principals, and parents are providing information to their children regarding alcohol and drug use. Thompson and Walters (2003) reported that teachers, principals, and parents are providing information to their children regarding alcohol and drug use. Their study found that fewer teens are using drugs because of the deliberate and serious messages they have received about the dangers of drug from their parents and leaders of prevention efforts. Parent's perceptions of their children's attitude of alcohol and substance use may present pertinent information not necessarily revealed by children.

According to a study conducted by the National Women's Health Resource Center (2005), peer pressure isn't the only major factor influencing whether teens use drugs. Parents also play an important role. The study found that much of the previous research in this area showed that adolescents make their decisions about drugs based on influence from their friends. The study also found that parents had a direct effect on lowering drug abuse, even in the face of peer influences.

Additionally, the study indicated that parents can make a difference in peer choices, or even after those peer choices are made, it an important message to get out there. It is important that parents stay strong and stick with their children regarding issues with substance use. Parents should not give up on their child during this time, even if they find out that their child is involved in issues facing substance use.

The study of more than 4,000 students in grades seven to twelve found that frequency of marijuana use declined 10 percent for each degree that teens perceive their parents are monitoring their activities, even after taking in to account peer influence and that risk of illegal drug use is reduced by 14 percent for each degree that teens believe parents are monitoring their activities

Little research has been conducted on parents' perception of adolescent's attitude of alcohol and substance abuse prevention programs, especially those comparing students' attitude of alcohol and substance abuse prevention programs. The research focuses on parent's beliefs of alcohol and substance abuse and teachers, principals and administrator's perceptions.

Overall the Partnership of Drug Free America research indicated broad views on the issues of parent's perception of their teen's attitudes regarding alcohol and substance use. Many factors, such as parent's knowledge and understanding of alcohol and substance use had created problems for teen's attitudes toward substance use.

Parents Perception of Substance Use by Ethnic Backgrounds

While an extensive body of literature has emerged in the past few decades on the subject of substance use, as well as ethnic backgrounds of adolescents, very little research currently exists on the parents' perception of their children's attitudes toward substance use by ethnic backgrounds.

Fortunately, the existing information on parent's perception is helpful in laying the foundation for further research work in this area of practice.

A review of research literature on parents' perception of adolescents' attitude toward substance use by differing ethnic backgrounds produced limited and mixed results. Most studies described parent's perception as effective in reducing the risk of youth use of alcohol and cigarettes, the extent to which these programs include parental participation is actually low, particularly for high risk-population (Journal of the National Medical Association, 2009).

In an effort to gather information on the racial and ethnic differences among parent's concern and perception of children drug use, Shijun Zhu et al., 2009 conducted a study supported by the National Institute on Drug Abuse. According to the Journal of the National Medical Association (2009) parental concern and negative attitudes toward drug use may prevent youth from being involved in drug use. However, few studies have addressed parental concern about children's drug use and its possible variation by race and ethnicity. The study found explored racial and ethnic differences among parent's perception and concern of children from a national sample. The study found that there were differences of ethnic groups among children.

The study also found that there were also differences among children's age, gender, poverty level and family structure. According to the Journal of the National Medical Associations (2009), clearly more research, particularly those in longitudinal nature is needed to clarify the ethnic role in associations of norms of parents on adolescents' drug use. If so, the findings of this study might shed light for school based youth drug use prevention programs for multiethnic populations

The statistical data in this study were from the 2003 National Survey of Children's Health, a random household survey of parents of children up to age 17. The analytic sample was restricted to parents of children aged 6 to 17 years (Journal of the National Medical Assoication, 2009).

As the Journal of National Medical Association (2009) noted:

> Among the total sample, approximately 21% of parents had a lot or a little concern about their children's

substance use. About 31% of parents of Hispanic children or adolescents had a lot or a little concern about their children's drug use, compared to 17% for their white counterparts, 20% for multiple race, and 26% for other racial and ethnic groups. Bivariate analyses indicated associations between parental concerns regarding drug use and age of the child, the gender of the child, family structure and family income. Parents of older age groups of adolescent had more concern about their children's drug use. Parents of African American and Hispanic children were more likely to express concern about their children's drug use than parents of white and other ethnic groups, even after adjusting for the confounding effects of other demographic or socioeconomic status (p.915).

The Journal of National Medical Association (2009) concluded that the level of parental concern about adolescent drug use was different across race and ethnicity groups. The results may have implications for parental participation in school-based adolescent prevention programs.

Summary

This research study has reviewed literature related to adolescents' attitudes toward substance use among differing ethnic backgrounds. Several themes emerged in this review. In response to the adolescent's attitudes toward substance use in the last few decades, research among the rise and fall of substance use is still needed.

This chapter gave an overview of pertinent empirical as well as theoretical literature on the subject of substance use including parents' perception. It appears that research in the area of parents' perception of their adolescent's attitude of substance use is surfacing; however, little is currently know about ramifications of parent perceptions regarding ethnic differences. The following chapter examined into the methodology for the current study which attempted to expand the knowledge base of this study. Specifically, the study focused on differing ethnic backgrounds of adolescents regarding substance use.

CHAPTER THREE

METHOD

Introduction

The preceding chapter gave a brief overview of empirical literature and research currently available on the subject of parents' perception of their children's attitude toward substance use by differing ethnic backgrounds. This chapter discussed the methodology that was utilized for the current study.

Research Design

This study was quantitative in nature using a comparative research design. A survey containing 206 questions of parents/guardians regarding their perceptions of adolescents' attitudes toward alcohol and substance use was administered. Sources of data were individual surveys conducted with parents and guardians that were current parents and or guardians of their adolescents.

According to Creswell (2003), a survey design provides a quantitative or numeric description of trends, attitudes, or opinions of a population by studying a sample or that population. From sample results, the researcher generalizes or makes claims about the population.

The researcher utilized a traditional quantitative design approach which entails recruitment of study participants for the individual's web-based survey that achieved through a purposeful sampling by random and informal snowball techniques. For example: the rationale for this method of sampling was based on the assumption that in order to discover understand and gain insight into the experiences of study participants, a researcher needs to select a sample from which the most can be learned.

McMillan & Schumacher (2001), outlined reasons for utilizing a quantitative approach. Designing a quantitative research involves choosing subjects, data collection techniques (such as questionnaires, observations, or interviews) procedures for gathering the data and procedures for implementing treatments together, these components constitute the methods part of the study.

Selection of Participants

The study participants were two-hundred six (206) parents who currently were legal guardians of adolescents. To qualify for this study, the parents/guardians had to have children between the ages of 12-17. The researcher attempted to recruit participants for the study by doing the following: first, the researcher attended existing PTA meeting at middle and high schools that took place in various places in the United States during the 2009 fiscal school year. The researcher sent out emails to various parents, guardians and counselors of children age 12-17.

Study participants consisted of parents in the United States who currently were either parent and or guardian of adolescents age 12-17. Recruitment of study participants for individual surveys was achieved by a random and informal "snowball" technique. The only criterion for inclusion in the study was that the individual were a parent or legal guardian of the adolescent who voluntary agreed to participate in the survey research study.

Instrumentation and Data Collection Strategies

To collect data, this study used "The You and Your School" survey created for a study by The Center for Substance Abuse Prevention (1993), supported by The National Clearinghouse for Alcohol and Drug Information. That study collected data from adolescents in grades 7-12 in Charleston South Carolina. According to Gottfreson (1990), the questionnaire measured factors associated with alcohol and substance use among teens. "The You and Your School" survey was a preliminary version of "What About You", a questionnaire designed to measure drug involvement and risk factors for later drug use.

The survey consisted of 10 scales and 4 sets of individual variable questions. The scales are (a) Belief in Pro-Social Norms, (b) Social Integration, (c) Commitment to School, (d) Rebellious Behavior, (e) Rebellious Behavior, (f) Peer Drug Modeling, (g)Attitudes Against Substance Use, (h) Attachment to School, (I) Self-Esteem, (j) Assertiveness, and (k) Positive Peer Modeling. The individual variable questions consisted of: (a) Attitudes about Police, (b) Coping with Stress, (c) Last Year Drug Use, and (d) Last Month Drug Use.

Harmon (1993) stated that scales of reliabilities were determined using Cronbach's alpha. The alpha used in the above-mentioned study consisted of .66. Each scale was calculated so that a high score indicates a high level of the factor. For all scales, the items were re coded so that the responses were in the same direction and averaged.

However, for the purpose of this research study, the researcher used four sets of scales from the survey consisting of 11 questions about attitude against substance use, 3 questions pertaining to peer drug modeling, 14 questions about self-esteem and 6 questions about positive peer modeling. The questions are answered with true or false, and yes/no. A series of 16 questions relating to demographic information was also used.

Procedure

Several procedures were used for this study. A survey was administered to parents/guardians of 7th to 12th grade students. Participants were recruited by the researcher through a mass emails. The snowball method was utilized, using PTA parents and parents of local communities of differing ethnic backgrounds. Individuals who were interested in participating were directed to an address on the worldwide web http://www.surveymonkey.com where they were able to access the on-line survey. After logging on, a letter of consent (see Appendix B) was presented. When participants signed and sent the letter of consent, they electronically completed and submit a 4-part questionnaire including demographic information.

Participants were recruited by the researcher, who sent out e-mails from a general list server that included middle school counselors personally known by the researcher using the snowball method. The snowball sampling was initially relied on subjects selected from a general list server by asking friends, family, counselors, PTA and community parents to participate in the study. Bryman (2004) stated that "snowball sampling is a form of conscience sample… with this approach to sampling: the researcher made initial contact with a group of people who were relevant to the research topic and then used them to established contact with others". To start the sampling process, the researcher emailed the above-mentioned potential participants to ask if they would be willing to participate. Once the researcher gained the first participant of the sample, it was then possible to ask if they were willing to introduce more people to the researcher.

Considering that the survey questions were about adolescents, each participant agreed to answer each survey question as if they felt their child would answer.

Data Analysis

The survey responses were coded prepared and analyzed using the statistical package for social sciences SPSS 15.0 software. ANOVA test was used to compare the differences of adolescent ethnic backgrounds. Once it was determined if differences exist among means (at least one group mean is different from another), a post hoc test may be utilized. However, considering that there were no differences among the varying ethnic groups, a post hoc test was not used to determine if group means were different.

In the final data analysis step, an excel spreadsheet was setup. Coded demographic and background information as well as coded survey responses were entered. The information was converted into SPSS file to get percentages.

The next chapter presents the results and finding derived from the data analysis gathered for the current study.

Assumptions of this Study

Three assumptions were identified for this research study.

1. Parents have connection with their children's attitudes regarding alcohol and substance use.

2. Parents' perceptions of their teens' attitudes can be measured.

3. The researcher attempted to understand the experiences of the participants (parents/guardians) by gathering the information from a web-based survey and making interpretations by the researcher's personal experiences and backgrounds with alcohol and substance use counseling.

CHAPTER FOUR

FINDINGS

Restatement of the Purpose

The purpose of this quantitative research was to examine parents' perceptions of adolescents' attitude towards substance use. Specifically, the study compared parent's perceptions of their teens' attitudes with regard to differing ethnic backgrounds. Parents play a vital role in their teens' attitudes toward substance use. The examination of parents' perception of adolescents' attitude regarding substance use helped to assist in determining if parent's perception can help children resist alcohol and substance use. The researchers' hope from this study was that parents can be more aware of their teen's attitude regarding substance use.

A survey was developed to identify parents' responses of their teen's attitudes regarding substance use, self-esteem, peer drug modeling and positive peer modeling (see Appendix A). This research study was conducted in order to determine whether parent's perception play a significant difference regarding adolescent's attitude regarding substance use by varying ethnic backgrounds.

Harmon (1993), developed "The You and Your School "survey created for a study by The Center for Substance Abuse (1993), supported by The National Clearinghouse for Alcohol and Drug Information. You and Your school was a preliminary version of What about You? (Gottfredson, 1990), a questionnaire designed to measure drug involvement and risk factors for later drug use.

For the purpose of this study, a total of 206 (n=206) respondents were randomly selected to make up the sample using a web-based survey. Selected participants answered a survey questionnaire on various scales regarding parent's perception of their adolescents' attitude toward substance use consisting of 50 questions. Data gathered were computed for interpretation. Response from the survey was analyzed using non-parametric tests, frequencies, percentages and one-way A Nova.

Demographics

The descriptive statistics for the participants' demographics are listed in Table 1. Each demographic variable was calculated into frequencies and percentages. Demographic survey question is listed in Appendix A. A majority (136, 67.0%) of the respondents were the mothers of the adolescents. The participants' ethnicity was reported as follows: 99 (48.3%) African-American, 56 (27.3%) European-American, 27 (13.2%) Hispanic, 17 (8.3%) Asian/Pacific Islander, 1 (0.5%) Native American/American Indian and 5 (2.4%) Other. Other represented a blank space to write down participants' ethnicity including multi ethnic groups. A large majority (182, 90.5%) of the participants described themselves as working class or middle class. Fifty-six (28.0%) of the participants indicated that they have a history of substance use, and 144 (72.0%) reported they have no history of substance use. Approximately half (95, 48.2%) of the respondents indicated that they have had experience with prevention programs. A majority (174, 85.7%) of the respondents stated that they had discussed substance use issues with their children, and most (182, 90.1%) revealed that they monitored their adolescents' daily activities. Twenty-eight (14.8%) of the participants reported that they worked part-time, and 129 (65.2%) stated that they worked full-time. Only 26 (13.1%) of the participants reported working from home.

Table 1

Descriptive Statistics for the Participants' Demographics

Variable	n	%
Race		
Black/African American	99	48.3
White/European American	56	27.3
Hispanic/Latino	27	13.2
Asian/Pacific Islander	17	8.3
Native American/American Indian	1	0.5
Other/Multi-Ethnic Groups	5	2.4

The participants also responded to several questions pertaining to their middle or high school students' demographics. The descriptive statistics for these responses are listed in Table 2. The average participant's adolescents' was 14.95 (SD = 2.18) years of age. The adolescents' ethnicity was reported as follows: 95 (46.8%) African-American, 53 (26.1%) European-American, 25 (12.3%) Hispanic, 16 (7.9%) Asian, 1 (0.5%) Native American and 13 (6.4%) Other. Other represented a blank space for participants to write down their ethnicity including multi-ethnic groups.

One-hundred twenty (58.3%) of the adolescents were female, and 86 (41.7%) were male. A majority (109, 53.7%) of the adolescents had a drug/alcohol awareness program at their school.

Table 2

Descriptive Statistics for the Adolescents' Demographics

Variable	n	%
Race		
Black/African American	95	46.8
White/European American	53	26.1
Hispanic/Latino	25	12.3
Asian/Pacific Islander	16	7.9
Native American/American Indian	1	0.5
Other/Multi-Ethnic Groups	13	6.4
Gender		
Female	120	58.3
Male	86	41.7
Child Grade		
7th Grade	35	17.20
8th Grade	29	14.2
9th Grade	25	12.3
10th Grade	44	21.6
11th Grade	16	7.8
12th Grade	55	27.0

Restatement of Purpose

The purpose of this study was to explore and solicit authentic feedback from parents/guardians, specifically of adolescent's attitude towards substance use by ethnic differences.

Analysis of Responses to Survey Questions

Following are the results from the analysis of the raw data from each of the five research questions that were posed to parent's perceptions of their adolescent's attitudes toward substance use by varying ethnic backgrounds.

Research Question 1a. Is there a statistically significant difference between the ethnic groups (African American vs. Caucasian vs. Hispanic vs. Other) on the parents' perceptions of their adolescents' attitudes towards substance use?

H_0: There will be no statistically significant difference between the ethnic groups (African American vs. Caucasian vs. Hispanic vs. Other) on the parents' perceptions of their adolescents' attitudes towards substance use.

A one-way ANOVA was conducted to determine if there was a significant difference between the ethnic groups on the parents' perceptions of their adolescents' attitudes towards substance use. The dependent variable was created with an additive composite score from the two items on page 5 of the survey. The items were coded for the computation as follows: yes = 2, maybe = 1, no = 0 (possible range: 0 – 4). The descriptive statistics for the individual items are listed in Appendix B.

The data was screened for outliers prior to analysis. The dependent variable was standardized by group, and the resulting z-scores were reviewed to determine if there were outliers in the data. Data points with a standardized score greater than |3| should be removed from the analysis. This process did not reveal any outliers in the data. Levene's test was not significant, suggesting that the groups had equal error variances.

The means and standard deviations of parent perceptions by ethnicity are listed in Table 3. The ANOVA (Table 4) failed to reveal a significant difference between the ethnic groups on the parents' perceptions of their adolescents' attitudes towards substance use, $F(3, 187) = 1.44, p > .05$ ($\eta^2 = .02$, power = .38). Bonferroni post hoc tests were not conducted because the ANOVA was not significant.

Table 3

Means and Standard Deviations of Parent Perceptions by Ethnicity

Race	M	SD	N
White/European American	1.83	0.70	53
Black/African American	1.98	0.73	92
Hispanic/Latino	2.13	0.46	23
Other	1.78	0.85	23

Table 4

One-way ANOVA on Parent Perceptions by Ethnicity

Source	SS	df	Mean Square	F	Sig.
Between Groups	2.17	3	0.72	1.44	.234
Within Groups	93.95	187	0.50		
Total	96.11	190			

<u>Research Question 1b.</u> Is there a statistically significant difference between the ethnic groups (African American vs. Caucasian vs. Hispanic vs. Other) on the parents' perceptions of their adolescents' attitudes towards substance use?

H_0: There will be no statistically significant difference between the ethnic groups (African American vs. Caucasian vs. Hispanic vs. Other) on the parents' perceptions of their adolescents' attitudes towards substance use.

A one-way ANOVA was conducted to determine if there was a significant difference between the ethnic groups on the parents' perceptions of their adolescents' attitudes towards substance use. The dependent variable was operationalized in a different manner for this analysis. The variable was created with an additive composite score from the nine items on page 6 of the survey. The items were coded for the computation as follows: yes = 1, no = 0 (possible range: 0 – 9). The descriptive statistics for the individual items are listed in Appendix C.

The data was screened for outliers prior to analysis. The dependent variable was standardized by group, and the resulting z-scores were reviewed to determine if there were outliers in the data. Data points with a standardized score greater than |3| should be removed from the analysis. This process did not reveal any outliers in the data. Levene's test was not significant, suggesting that the groups had equal error variances.

The means and standard deviations of parent perceptions by ethnicity are listed in Table 5. The ANOVA (Table 6) failed to reveal a significant difference between the racial groups on the parents' perceptions of their adolescents' attitudes towards substance use, $F(3, 177) = 1.38, p > .05$ ($\eta^2 = .02$, power = .36). Bonferroni post hoc tests were not conducted because the ANOVA was not significant.

Table 5

Means and Standard Deviations of Parent Perceptions by Ethnicity

Race	M	SD	N
White/European American	3.63	1.84	46
Black/African American	3.76	1.69	92
Hispanic/Latino	4.09	1.44	23
Other	3.05	1.99	20

Table 6

One-way ANOVA on Parent Perceptions by Ethnicity

Source	SS	Df	Mean Square	F	Sig.
Between Groups	12.44	3	4.15	1.38	.251
Within Groups	532.23	177	3.01		
Total	544.67	180			

<u>Research Question 2.</u> Is there a statistically significant difference between the ethnic groups (African American vs. Caucasian vs. Hispanic vs. Other) on the parents' perceptions of their adolescents' attitudes/perceptions of peer drug modeling?

H_0: There will be no statistically significant difference between the ethnic groups (African American vs. Caucasian vs. Hispanic vs. Other) on the parents' perceptions of their adolescents' attitudes/perceptions of peer drug modeling.

A one-way ANOVA was conducted to determine if there was a significant difference between the ethnic groups on the parents' perceptions of their adolescents' attitudes/perceptions of peer drug modeling. The dependent variable was operationalized with an additive composite score from the 3 items on page 9 of the survey. The items were coded for the computation as follows: true = 1, false = 0 (possible range: 0 – 3). The descriptive statistics for the individual items are listed in Appendix D.

The data was screened for outliers prior to analysis. The dependent variable was standardized by group, and the resulting z-scores were reviewed to determine if there were outliers in the data. Data points with a standardized score greater than |3| should be removed from the analysis. This process did not reveal any outliers in the data. Levene's test was not significant, suggesting that the groups had equal error variances.

The means and standard deviations of parent perceptions of peer drug modeling by ethnicity are listed in Table 7. The ANOVA (Table 8) failed to reveal a significant difference between the ethnic groups on the parents' perceptions of their adolescents' attitudes/perceptions of peer drug modeling, $F(3, 184) = 1.93$, $p > .05$ ($\eta^2 = .03$, power = .49). Bonferroni post hoc tests were not conducted because the ANOVA was not significant.

Table 7

Means and Standard Deviations of Parent Perceptions of Peer Drug Modeling by Ethnicity

Race	M	SD	N
White/European American	0.85	0.92	52
Black/African American	0.72	0.86	90
Hispanic/Latino	1.09	0.95	23
Other	1.13	0.87	23

Table 8

One-way ANOVA on Parent Perceptions by Ethnicity

Source	SS	df	Mean Square	F	Sig.
Between Groups	4.57	3	1.52	1.93	.126
Within Groups	145.26	184	0.79		
Total	149.83	187			

Research Question 3. Is there a statistically significant difference between the ethnic groups (African American vs. Caucasian vs. Hispanic vs. Other) on the parents' perceptions of their adolescents' self-esteem?

H_0: There will be no statistically significant difference between the ethnic groups (African American vs. Caucasian vs. Hispanic vs. Other) on the parents' perceptions of their adolescents' self-esteem.

A one-way ANOVA was conducted to determine if there was a significant difference between the ethnic groups on the parents' perceptions of their adolescents' self-esteem.

The dependent variable was operationalized with an additive composite score from the 14 items on pages 10 and 11 of the survey. The items were coded for the computation as follows: true = 1, false = 0 (possible range: 0 – 14). The descriptive statistics for the individual items are listed in Appendix E.

The data was screened for outliers prior to analysis. The dependent variable was standardized by group, and the resulting z-scores were reviewed to determine if there were outliers in the data. Data points with a standardized score greater than |3| should be removed from the analysis. This process revealed 3 outliers in the data. Levene's test was not significant, suggesting that the groups had equal error variances.

The means and standard deviations of parent perceptions of their adolescents' self-esteem by ethnicity are listed in Table 9. The ANOVA (Table 10) failed to reveal a significant difference between the ethnic groups on the parents' perceptions of their adolescents' self-esteem, $F(3, 158) = 0.85$, $p > .05$ ($\eta^2 = .02$, power = .23). Bonferroni post hoc tests were not conducted because the ANOVA was not significant.

Table 9

Means and Standard Deviations of Parent Perceptions of Self-Esteem by Ethnicity

Race	M	SD	N
White/European American	8.13	1.70	40
Black/African American	8.19	1.32	81
Hispanic/Latino	7.79	1.84	19
Other	8.59	2.22	22

Table 10

One-way ANOVA on Parent Perceptions by Ethnicity

Source	SS	df	Mean Square	F	Sig.
Between Groups	6.74	3	2.25	0.85	.468
Within Groups	417.07	158	2.64		
Total	423.81	161			

Research Question 4. Is there a statistically significant difference between the ethnic groups (African American vs. Caucasian vs. Hispanic vs. Other) on the parents' perceptions of their adolescents' positive peer modeling?

H_0: There will be no statistically significant difference between the ethnic groups (African American vs. Caucasian vs. Hispanic vs. Other) on the parents' perceptions of their adolescents' positive peer modeling.

A one-way ANOVA was conducted to determine if there was a significant difference between the ethnic groups on the parents' perceptions of their adolescents' positive peer modeling. The dependent variable was operationalized with an additive composite score from the 5 items on page 12 of the survey. The items were coded for the computation as follows: not important at all = 0, important = 1, very important = 2 (possible range: 0 – 10). The descriptive statistics for the individual items are listed in Appendix F.

The data was screened for outliers prior to analysis. The dependent variable was standardized by group, and the resulting z-scores were reviewed to determine if there were outliers in the data. Data points with a standardized score greater than |3| should be removed from the analysis. This process did not reveal any outliers in the data. Levene's test was not significant, suggesting that the groups had equal error variances.

The means and standard deviations of parent perceptions of their adolescents' self-esteem by ethnicity are listed in Table 11. The ANOVA (Table 12) failed to reveal a significant difference between the ethnic groups on the parents' perceptions of their adolescents' positive peer modeling, $F(3, 173) = 1.27$, $p > .05$ ($\eta^2 = .02$, power = .34). Bonferroni post hoc tests were not conducted because the ANOVA was not significant.

Table 11
Means and Standard Deviations of Parent Perceptions of Positive Peer Modeling by Ethnicity

Race	M	SD	N
White/European American	8.38	2.05	50
Black/African American	7.90	2.42	87
Hispanic/Latino	7.30	2.20	20
Other	8.30	2.23	20

Table 12
One-way ANOVA on Parent Perceptions by Ethnicity

Source	SS	df	Mean Square	F	Sig.
Between Groups	19.73	3	6.58	1.27	.286
Within Groups	896.25	173	5.18		
Total	915.98	176			

Summary

This chapter has presented the results of the quantitative analyses performed to address the purpose of this study, findings about the parent's perceptions of their adolescent's attitude toward substance use. The present study showed that significant differences did not exist between parent's perceptions of their adolescent's attitudes toward substance use as measured by ethnic differences, self-esteem, positive peer modeling and peer drug modeling.

CHAPTER FIVE

DISCUSSION, RECOMMENDATION AND SUMMARY

Discussion of Study and Purpose Justification

In this research study, Chapters, One, Two, Three and Four addressed the purpose, problem, methodology and findings of this research. The purpose of this quantitative research study was to examine parent's perceptions of their adolescents' attitude toward substance use and other related demographic factors. Specifically, the study compared parent's perception with regard to differing ethnic backgrounds. The development of the survey was in conjunction with parameters set by The You and Your Survey created by the Center for Substance Abuse Prevention (1993).

Several procedures were used for this study. A survey was administered to parents/guardians of 7th to 12th grade students regarding varying ethnic backgrounds. Participants were recruited by the researcher by email. The snowball method was utilized, using parents in the PTA and parents of local communities of differing ethnic backgrounds. Individuals who were interested in participating were directed to an address of the worldwide web http://www.surveymonkey.com where they were able to access the on-line survey. Data was reported in terms of frequencies and percentages and analyzed through the use of a one-way ANOVA.

The survey was created and administered to evaluate parent's perceptions of their adolescents' attitudes toward substance use. Results obtained illustrated no statistically significant relationships regarding parent's perceptions of their adolescents' attitude toward substance use relating to self-esteem, peer drug modeling and positive drug modeling between the varying ethnic backgrounds.

A one-way ANOVA was conducted to determine if there was a significant difference between the different ethnic groups on the parents' perceptions of their adolescents' attitudes towards substance use. A Boneferroni post hoc test were not conducted because the ANOVA test was not significant. The results from the study proved that there are no differences among the varying ethnic groups regarding adolescents' attitude towards substance use. From the study, it is clear that parent's' views regarding substance use issues among adolescents showed no statistically significant difference among the varying ethnic groups.

A descriptive survey was designed and sent in April 2009 to parents of adolescents regarding their attitudes toward substance use by ethnic differences. Approximately, 206 parents/guardians filled out and returned the questionnaire through a web-based survey. Much of the survey included demographic information relating to information pertaining to substance use issues. A fairly distributed number of parents/guardian returned the survey. The majority (136, 67.0%) of the respondents were the mothers of the adolescents, while (41, 20.20%) were fathers and (26, 12.8%) were considered others. The data also indicated that (56, 144.0 %) of the parents had experience substance use and (144, 72.0%) had no experience at all.

Interpretation of Data

The purpose of Chapter Five was to summarize the major findings, implications and recommendations further study. It was hypothesized that over the course of the study participants regarding adolescents' attitude towards substance would have a significant difference among parents and guardians. It was further hypothesized that over the course of the study, there would be a significant difference among the varying ethnic groups.

Unexpectedly, all of the hypotheses were not supported in this study. There were no significant differences found in parents' perceptions of their adolescent's attitude toward substance use by varying ethnic groups.

In response to the hypotheses, the following research questions were addressed in this study:

1. Is there a statistically significant difference between the ethnic groups (African American vs. Caucasian vs. Hispanic vs. Other/Mixed Ethnic Groups) on the parents' perception of their adolescents' attitudes towards substance use?

2. Is there a statistically significant difference between the ethnic groups (African American vs. Caucasian vs. Hispanic vs. Other/Mixed Ethnic Groups) on parents' perceptions of their adolescents of peer drug modeling?

3. Is there a statistically significant difference between the ethnic groups (African American vs. Caucasian vs. Hispanic vs. Other/Mixed Ethnic Groups) on the parents' perceptions of their adolescents' positive peer modeling?

4. Is there a statistically significant difference between the ethnic groups? (African American vs. Caucasian vs. Hispanic vs. Other/Mixed Ethnic Groups) on the parents' perceptions of their adolescents' positive peer modeling?

Demographic Profile

A profile was compiled from responses that represent the highest number of endorsement obtained from the survey. The majority of the respondents were the mothers of the adolescents. The participants' ethnicity was reported as follows: 99 (48.3%) were African-Americans, 56 (27.3%) European-American, 27 (13.2%) Hispanic, 1 (0.5%) Native American and 5(2.4%) Other. The average participant's adolescent was 14.95 (SD=2.18) years of age. The adolescents' ethnicity was reported as follows: 95 (46.9%) African-American, 53 (26.1%) European-American, 25 (12.3%) Hispanic, 16 (7.9%) Asian, 1 (0.5%) Native American and 13 (6.4%) Other (mixed ethnic background). One- hundred twenty (58.3%) of the adolescents were female, and 86 (41.7%) were male.

Additionally, this investigation supported the finding that the majority (174, 85.7%) of the respondents stated that they had discussed substance use issues with them children, and most (182, 90.1%) revealed that they monitored their adolescent's daily activities. Twenty-eight (14.8%) of the participants reported that they worked part-time, and 129 (65.2%) stated that they worked full-time. Only 26 (13.1%) of the participants reported working from home.

Discussion of Key Themes

Analysis of data from the current study produced four primary themes. These themes are discussed her in relation to how they fit with the findings from past literature review and research on parents' perception of their adolescent's attitude towards substance use by differing ethnic groups were employed.

The researcher believes that parent's perception is a very important factor regarding adolescent's attitude of substance use. A review of past research and empirical literature in the field of adolescent' attitude toward substance use showed that there was a need for more studies on the views of parents' perception by differing ethnic groups. Past studies also indicated that compared to parents in 1988, those in 2004 were significantly less likely to see great risks for their teens in using marijuana regular (Pasierb, 2004).

Research suggests that many parents may underestimate their importance as parents in terms of influence on their adolescent attitude regarding substance use. Parents/guardians attitude and their acceptance of adolescence substance use may range from denial and lack of knowledge and awareness of teens substance use issues. Parents often acknowledge their responsibilities to provide norms and boundaries for substance use within the parent-child relationship, but are commonly at a loss as to how to take the primary acting role of responsibility in this area (Gaves et al, 2005).

Analysis of data from the current study produced four primary themes. These themes are discussed her in relation to how they fit with findings from past literature review and research on parents' perceptions and ethnic differences among adolescent's attitude towards substance use. For the current study, Table 1 and 2 describes descriptive statistics for participant's demographics. For the current study, Table 1 indicated the descriptive statistics for the participants' demographics.

A profile was compiled from responses that represent the highest number of endorsement obtained from the survey. The majority of the respondents were the mothers of the adolescents. The participants' ethnicity was reported as follows: 99 (48.3%) were African-Americans, 56 (27.3%) European-American, 27 (13.2%) Hispanic, 1 (0.5%) Native American and 5(2.4%) Other. The average participant's adolescent was 14.95 (SD=2.18) years of age. The adolescents' ethnicity was reported as follows: 95 (46.9%) African-American, 53 (26.1%) European-American, 25 (12.3%) Hispanic, 16 (7.9%) Asian, 1 (0.5%) Native American and 13 (6.4%) Other (mixed ethnic background). One-hundred twenty (58.3%) of the adolescents were female, and 86 (41.7%) were male.

Additionally, this investigation supported the finding that the majority (174, 85.7%) of the respondents stated that they had discussed substance use issues with their children, and most (182, 90.1%) revealed that they monitored their adolescent's daily activities. Twenty-eight (14.8%) of the participants reported that they worked part-time, and 129 (65.2%) stated that they worked full-time. Only 26 (13.1%) of the participants reported working from home.

The first theme to emerge from the current study was parents' perception of their teen's attitudes toward substance use. Although the study did not show a significant difference among parent's/guardians perceptions, their views were a major contributing factor in this research study.

The research literature on parent's perception of their adolescents' attitudes toward substance use in this study indicates mixed results. Ross (1991) stated that gender information particularly with respect to the use of alcohol and cigarettes of boys and girls found that students who report they have used any alcohol numbered 42 percent; intent to use numbered 68 percent.

Recommendations were made for K-12 comprehensive prevention programs and for further research. Furthermore, within group comparisons the study shows a significant relationship to use alcohol and cigarettes among gender and grade levels.

For substance use, the one-way ANOVA failed to reveal a significant difference of parent's perceptions of adolescents' attitudes toward substance use. The examination of the effect size suggested that the effect was very small. The difference only accounted for 2% of the variance ($\eta^2=.02$). Overall, the results produced no meaningful differences regarding substance use among the varying ethnic groups. Bonferroni post hoc tests were not conducted because the ANOVA was not significant.

Table 3 presents the means and standard deviations for the variables used in the analysis, and correlations with selected independent variables.

Although research and information on adolescent's attitude toward substance use is surfacing, it is important to remember that parent's perception is a vital aspect regarding substance use among adolescents. While research as to whether parent's perceptions should be used to determine if adolescent's attitudes toward substance use by ethnic differences are still somewhat inconclusive, parent's perception may be helpful in many ways. It is important to recognize that many of the studies discussed in this study are incomplete or meager. This unexpected finding may be due in part to the fundamental belief that parents and guardians may feel that their children won't participate in alcohol and drug use.

The second theme to emerge from the current study was parent's perception of their adolescent's attitude toward substance use of peer drug modeling.

Ethnic differences were examined to determine if parent's perception regarding adolescent's attitudes of peer drug modeling showed a significant difference. There were no differences in peer drug modeling between ethnic groups. Responses to three parent's perception questions about peer drug modeling showed no significant differences among the varying ethnic groups. This leads to the conclusion that parent's perception regarding peer drug modeling, does not change the attitudes of adolescents regarding different ethnic groups. When examining parent's perception towards the particular data collection and analysis, there was no significant ($p>.05$) difference between the groups. Bonferroni post hoc tests were not conducted because the ANOVA was not significant.

There are several possible reasons for this tendency of the groups to answer differently. The first reason is simply that the parents did not like answering questions pertaining peer drug modeling regarding their child's friend. In some cases, the parent/guardian may not know who their child's friends are. Therefore, it may be hard to answers questions not specifically relating directly to the parent's child.

It is very reasonable to assume that parents/guardians did not like answering questions pertaining to other children. Replacing traditional data collection and analysis with peer drug modeling did not change parent's overall perception toward adolescents attitude.

The research literature reviewed that there were no significant differences among ethnic groups, but it showed that non-Hispanic origin adolescent had higher rates of substance use than African-American.

This study found that there was a small percentage of Native American and other ethnical groups that provided their input in the study. Specifically, Native American 1 (0.5%) and Hispanic 5 (2.4%) participated in the survey. In spite these differences, there were no differences found between the parent's perceptions of their adolescents' attitudes toward substance by ethnic differences.

The third theme to emerge from the current study was parents' perception of adolescent's attitudes towards substance use regarding self-esteem.

Attitudes were examined to determine parent's perception of their adolescents' self-esteem toward substance use of varying ethnic groups. There were no differences in adolescents' attitudes regarding self-esteem toward substance use from a parent's perception. Responses to fourteen questions about adolescents' attitudes of substance use regarding self-esteem showed no significant differences between parents' perceptions.

This leads to the conclusion that parent's perceptions for data collection and analysis does not change student's attitudes about substance use regarding self-esteem.

Conclusions drawn from this research suggest that parent's views regarding substance use issues among adolescents showed no significant difference among varying ethnic groups. While the majority of parents do support adolescent's attitude toward substance use, they believe that their children for the most part have a positive attitude regarding substance use. One of the greatest arguments against parents' perceptions of their child's attitudes towards substance use is that parents may view their children as doing no wrong when it comes to substance use. Parents believe that they are more informed about substance use now than ten years again. The Partnership for a Drug-Free America (2004), found that compared to parents in 1998, those in 2004 were significantly less likely to see great risk for their teens regarding substance use.

The final theme to emerge in this study was parents' perceptions of adolescent's substance use by ethnic differences regarding positive peer drug modeling. Parents are part of adolescents' everyday life and parent's perceptions of their child's attitudes toward substance is a vital part of this research study. According to The National Survey of American Attitudes on Substance Abuse (1996), most parents know, at some level, when their kids are at risk—the issues is whether they will act on their intuitions in a purposeful manner to reduce their teen's risk of drug use, rather than hide behind a vale of non-responsibility and inefficacy.

There were no differences in parents' perceptions of their adolescent's attitude toward substance use by ethnic differences. Responses to the survey questions about substance use, self-esteem, peer drug modeling and ethnic groups showed not significant differences between the groups. This leads to the conclusion in this study that parents' perceptions do not change adolescent's attitude toward substance use. There are several possible reasons for a non-significant different in this research study. The first reason is simply that the parents in this study may not be knowledgeable or confident about alcohol and drug use regarding their child's attitude towards substance use.

The Partnership for a Drug-Free America and MetLife Foundation (2008) states that parents need to feel that they have the knowledge and the ability to affect their child's behavior. It's critical to the effective prevention and cessation of teen drug and alcohol use that parents understand the importance of their role, that they employ a few basic parenting practices, and that they're aware of the risks of drug and alcohol use and communicate those risks to their children.

According to the Partnership for a Drug Free America (2003), given that parents of teens severely underestimate both the risk their teen sees in trying drugs and their friends' use of drugs; it should not be surprising that very few parents think their teens has tried drugs. While most teens have not tried drugs, teens are still far more likely to have tried drugs than their parents think.

Study Limitation

This research study looked at the factors associated with parent's perception of adolescent's attitudes toward substance use by varying ethnic backgrounds. Although this research resulted in some important finding, there were some important limitations.

First, the sample population selected for the research was a hard to reach target group using the world-wide web. This resulted in the need to open up and expand the individual parents/guardians sample. The survey study was limited due to the fact that a large number of participants did not have access to a computer, did not know how to use a computer and in some cases the computer did not work.

The second limiting factor was the selection of participants for the study. Although parents/guardians played a major role in the selection process of the study, it is important to note that the questions presented in the study could have also included the perceptions of adolescents. The study was limited only to those parents and guardians who were involved in their teen's lives regarding substance use. Furthermore, the sample was limited to parent's perceptions of students in 7th to 12th grade. Comparisons among parents-vs.-adolescents regarding attitudes of substance use may have presented different results. Based on the findings of the research, the design questions, while yielding important results, could be modified to enhance the overall results of the study.

Based on the finding of the survey implemented in this research study, it is evident that parents have both negative and positive feelings about their kids regarding substance use among varying ethnic backgrounds. Additionally, the study also seemed to indicate that parents have wishful thinking about their children; and that most parents seem to think that their child had little or no experience with substance use.

Implications

Given the large number of children and adolescents in America today, they are still experiencing issues with alcohol and substance use, however, it is important that communities around the world get involved with issues regarding adolescent's substance use. It is also critical that counseling practitioners, parents, schools, principals and school administrators educate themselves regarding substance use.

Findings from the current research study showed that the majority of (136, 67%) of the respondents were mothers of the adolescent. The current study identified an area of need for supportive services including fathers of adolescents with regard to substance use issues.

As the Partnership for a Drug-Free America (2008) noted:

> While it is encouraging that parents' feel more confident they can keep their children away from drugs and drinking, there is still room for improvement and more work to be done. In particular, fathers reported greater difficulty reconciling the desire to have their child see them as a friend with the need to set rules and monitor their teens. There is an opportunity for more fathers to recognize their important role in prevention and to engage more with their children on this important issue. By educating their teens about the specific drugs and their consequences, they will be better able to thoroughly educate them and make strides toward keeping their teens healthy. Adolescents can be particularly vulnerable to alcohol and drug abuse in periods of transition such as entering middle school or high school, or moving to a new town and a new school. Parents should be especially attentive to their child's moods and behavior at these times, and be particularly

alert for opportunities to initiate conversations about the risks of alcohol and drug use.

Recommendations

Findings from this study suggest a number of recommendations for parent's perception of adolescent's attitude toward substance use by varying ethnic backgrounds. The recommendations are organized around the major findings of the research study.

One of the most consistent and significant findings from parent's perceptions of adolescent's attitude toward substance use among varying ethnic differences survey was the need regarding outreach of ethnic backgrounds regarding substance use comparing both parents, guardians and adolescent perceptions regarding substance use. This could increase the knowledge and information of both parents and adolescents about substance use around the world.

One marketing strategy might be to plan and implement on-going informational marketing regarding the comparison of adolescent's and parent's perceptions. The parent's perception survey found that there is a need for additional services, particularly as it relates to the varying ethnic backgrounds of adolescent's attitudes toward substance use. The development and implementation of additional studies would augment what is currently available and would lead to a more comprehensive approach to the knowledge of substance use among ethnic groups.

The most surprising and revealing finding from this research was that approximately half (95, 48.2%) of the respondents indicated that they have had experience with prevention programs. This becomes an extremely important finding because it is the basis for current and future services of substance prevention and education around the world. This recommendation should be taken into consideration when planning, developing and implementing services and programs regarding substance use among adolescents.

Also, this revelation should motivate adolescents, parents, guardians and communities to acknowledge the importance of adolescent substance use with resources offered to assist them in their prevention program efforts.

Parents influence operates as a natural harm-reduction mechanism. Parents influence their children's drinking in many ways. Through family interactions, modeling and reinforcing standards and attitudes that children learn and use to guide their behavior in new situations, thus parental influence endure (Project Cork Organization, n.d.).

Recommendations for Future Research

The findings from this study indicated internal and external factors impacting the provision of parent's perception of adolescent's attitude toward substance use by varying racial backgrounds. These finding contribute to future policy development. Further research based upon these findings is needed to further examine the ways in which other selected individual variables/factors impact on decisions and practices of perceptions of adolescent's attitudes regarding substance use and ethnic differences. An example of this would be to examine the relationships of need regarding adolescents and parent's perceptions of Hispanic and Native American regarding substance use.

From this current study, the participants' ethnicity reported very low participations among Hispanic, 1 (0.5%) and Native American 5 (2.4%). The design, development and implementation of outreach strategies to potentially increase of the varying ethnic services would shed some light on how to better outreach different ethnic communities around the world. Future research could investigate and delineate possible demographic relationships or associations that may have influenced parent's responses.

Considering that approximately half of the parents in this study have had experience with prevention programs, it would be important for educators, counselors, schools and community to involve the parents when developing and planning alcohol and substance use prevention for adolescents.

Summary

Chapter one of this research study introduced and provided an overview of parents' perception of adolescents' attitudes toward substance use by varying ethnic backgrounds. This included discussing various aspects of parents' perception which included demographics, substance use, self-esteem, drug modeling and positive peer drug modeling and the identification for the specific framing, design and method of conducting this research study.

The problem statement, background, purpose, nature of the study, hypothesis and research questions all provided important context for the purpose of the research. Some of the benefits as well as challenges experienced by parents/guardians regarding adolescent's attitudes toward substance use were also discussed.

The chapter gave a brief review of parent's perception of adolescent's substance use.

According to The Project Cork (nod.), parents and teens often see the same things differently. Parents were more likely to attribute drug use to factor with negative connotation (such as boredom, rebellion, loneliness or social pressure). Their children were more likely to mention things with more positive connotation (such as curiosity, fun, insight or experience).

Research suggests that many parents may underestimate their importance as parent in terms of influence on their adolescents' attitude of substance use.

Parents/guardian attitude an acceptance of adolescent's substance use may range from denial and lack of knowledge and awareness of teen's substance use (Graves, 2005).

This was a study of the parent's perception of their adolescent's attitude toward substance use by varying ethnic backgrounds. In chapter one, the researcher introduced problems associated with alcohol and substance use among adolescent including ethnic differences.

Chapter two presented a review of literature on the subject of parent's perception of their adolescent's attitude toward substance by ethnic differences. The chapter also gave a brief review of adolescent's attitude toward substance use, adolescent's attitude toward substance use among minority groups, parent's perception of adolescent's attitude toward substance use and parent's perception of substance use by ethnic backgrounds. This investigation into these areas was conducted through internet sources, peer review journals, articles, other academic materials and professional materials.

Chapter three described the research methodology, design, and procedures data processing and analysis utilized for the study. The chapter also described the methodology, hypotheses, and research questions. Also, the specific and necessary steps to implement a research study of this nature were outlined in this chapter.

Chapter four presented the results of the current study based on the analysis of the raw data that was obtained from the survey presented to parents and guardian. The reporting of the results and key findings of the research described the major themes of the research. A descriptive analysis was also conducted for all possible similarities comparisons and contrast of independent and dependent variables.

Finally, this chapter presented a discussion of the study purposes and justification, the four research questions that emerged from the data analysis, study limitations, implications for practice and recommendation for future research.

Chapter five provided the discussions for the conclusion and recommendation for the research study. This chapter described the findings and conclusions from the study.

Also, included in this chapter were the significance of the study recommendation and direction for future research.

REFERENCES

Alcohol Policies Project (2005). Advocacy for the Prevention of Alcohol Problems: Young People Alcohol.

Botvin, G.J., (2006). National Institute on Drug Abuse. Preventing Drug Abuse through the Schools: Intervention Programs that Work.

Carolyn C.J., Kurt J.G., Larry S. W., & Gerald S.B., (2004). Journal of child and family studies. Alcohol first use and attitudes among young children, 6(3), 359-372.

Center for Substance Abuse Prevention (1993). Prevention strategies based on individual risk factors for alcohol and other drug abuse. Rockville, MD: U. S. Department of Health and Human Services Administration

Center for Alcohol and Substance Abuse (2006). Teen Survey Reveals: Teen Parties Awash in Alcohol, Marijuana and Illegal Drugs—Even When Parents Are Present. Retrieved February 5, 2008, from http://www.casacolumbia.org

Creswell, J.W. (2003). Research design, Qualitative, Quantitative, and mixed methods approaches (2nd ed.). Thousand Oaks, CA: Sage Publications.

Delaney, B., (2002). Partnership for a Drug-Free America: Partnership Attitude Tracking Study. Teens: Ethnic and Racial Trends, Spring 2002. Retrieved January 7, 2008 from http://www.drugfreeamerica.org/Home/Default.asp?

Donnermeyer, J.F. (2000). Parents' Perception of School Based Prevention
Education. Journal of Drug Education, 30(3), 325-342

Drug Use in the General U. S. Population (2006). World Almanac & Book of Facts; 2008, 135-136.

Education Resources Information Center (1983). Weekly Reader Publications, Middletown, CT. A Study of Children's Attitudes and Perceptions about Drugs and Alcohol.

French, K., Finkbiner, R., & Duhamel, L. (2002). Patterns of Substance Use Among Minority Youth and Adults in the United States: An

Overview and Synthesis of National Survey Findings, VA: Caliber Associates.

Friedman, A., & Utada, A. (1992). The Family Environment of Adolescent Drug Abuse.

Gans, S., (2002). Survey on American Attitudes on Substance Abuse. The National Survey of Americans Attitudes on Substance Abuse.

Gans, S., (2007). About.com: Alcoholism. Health's Disease and Condition. Retrieved from http://alcoholism.about.com/b/2007/11/01/most-parents-are-aware-of-teens-substance-abuse.

Harmon, M.A., (1993). Drug Abuse Resistance Education. The You and Your School Evaluation Review, (17) 221-239.

Johnston, L. D., Bachman, J. G., & O'Malley, M. (1990). Monitoring the future: A continuing study of the lifestyles and values of youth. Ann Arbor, MI: The University of Michigan Institute for Social Research.

Johnston, LD., O'Malley, P.M., & Bachman, J. G. (1999). National survey results on drug use from The Monitoring the Future Study (pp. 1975-1977). Rockville, MD: National Institute on Drug Abuse.

Johnston, L., Bachman, J., & O'Malley J. (1999). Monitoring the Future: National Results on Adolescent Drug Use. Overview of Key Findings. (Washington, D.C: NIDA, 2000, pp.3-6).

Johnston, L.D., et al. (2005). Monitoring the Future national results on adolescent drug use: Overview of key findings, 2004 (NIH Publication No. 05-5726), pp.1-66. Bethesda, MD: National Institute on Drug Abuse

Joseph, A., (2005). National Survey of American Attitudes of Substance Abuse Teens and Parents. The National Center on Addiction and Substance Abuse at Columbia University. The National Center on Addiction and Substance Abuse at Columbia University.

Lynda K., (2004). United States Department of Health and Human Services and SAMHSA's National Clearinghouse for Alcohol and Drug Information (2002).

McMillan, J.H., & Schumacher, S. (2001). Research in Education. A Conceptual Introduction (5th ed., pp. 165). Library of Congress Cataloging-in Publication Data

National Household Survey on Substance Abuse. (1996). Rockville, MD: Substance Abuse and Mental Health Services Administration (SAMHSA)

National Household Survey on Drug Abuse. (1999). Office of Applied Studies. Youth Substance Use. Retrieved from http://www.oas.samhsa.gov/NHSDA/99

National Survey of American Attitudes towards Alcohol and Substance Abuse: II Teens and their Parents. (1996). New York: National Center on Addiction and Substance Abuse (CASA**).**

National Household on Drug Use and Health (2007). Youth Drug Use at a Five-Year High.

Payne, K. (2002). British Medical Association BMA, article Alcohol and Young People, Health 1999. Prevention Alert, Volume 5 Number 6. Retrieved November 1, 2209, from www.nacadi.samhsa.gov/govpubs/prevalert/v5/2.aspx

Substance Abuse and Mental Health Services Administration (2006). United States Department of Health. Drug Use in the General Population, World Almanac and Book Facts; pp.136.

National Household on Drug Use and Health (2005). Binge Alcohol Use among Persons Ages 12-20: 2002 and 2003 update Office of Applied Studies, Substance Abuse and Mental Health Services Administration. (2003). Results from the 2002 National Survey on Drug Use And Health: National Findings (DHHS Publication No. SMA 03-3836, NHSDA Series H-22). Rockville, MD: Substance Abuse and Mental Health Services

Partnership Attitude Tracking Study (PATS), Teen Study. (1997). New York: Partnership For A Drug-Free America.

Partnership for a Drug-Free America (PDFA). (1994). Inhalants Research Interviews with Children Ages 9-15 and Parents of Children Ages 6-17. New York: PDFA.

Partnership for a Drug-Free America (PDFA). (1995). Young Teens and Marijuana: Defining our Primary Target. New York: PDFA.

Partnership for a Drug-Free America (PDFA). (1996). Marijuana Strategic Study: Promise Test. New York: PDFA.

Partnership for a Drug-Free America (2008). Partnership Attitude Tracking Study 2008. MetLife Foundation.

Pasierb, S. (2005). New National Study Reveals Drug Experienced Parents see less risk. Talk with teens about drugs.

Roper. A.S., (2003). Partnership Attitude Tracking Study Teen Study. Survey of Teen's Attitudes and Behaviors toward Marijuana.

Ross, J.P., (1991). Alcohol and other drugs attitudes and use among suburban fifth and sixth-grade students 52, 2817-2828.

Ruderstam, K. E. & Newton, R.R., (2007). Surviving your Dissertation.

A Comprehensive Guide to Content and Process (3rd e.d.). Sage Publications, Inc., 328.

Shijun, Z., Wang, Y., Browne, D., & Wagner, F. (2009). Journal of the National Medical Association. Racial/Ethnic Differences in Parental Concern about Their Child's Drug Use in a Nationally Representative Sample in the United States, 915-919.

Sloboda, Z., & Stephens, R., (2001). University of Akron Institute for Health and Social Policy. Major Drug Prevention Program.

Substance Abuse and Mental Health Services Administration (1999). Office of Applied Studies, U. S. Department of Human Services Retrieved October 31, 2009, from http://www.drugabusestatitistics.samhsa.gov Substance Abuse and Mental Health Services Administration (2003). Office of Applied Studies, Nation Household on Drug Abuse, 21 DHS Publication (3) 374. Rockville MD Retrieved November 12, 2007, from http://ncdi.samhsa.gov/govpubs/F036/monograph1.aspx

Substance Abuse and Mental Health Services Administration (2003). Overview of Findings from the 2002 National Survey on Drug Use and Health. Office of Applied Studies, NHSDA Series H-21. Rockville, MD.

Substance Abuse and Mental Health Services Administration (2009). The National Center on Addiction and Substance Abuse. Study: Painkiller Misuse Up Among Young Adults.

Substance Abuse and Mental Health Services Administration (2009). About Teens.com. Annual Household Survey Finds Millions of Americans in Denial about Drug Abuse. Retrieved December 12, 2009 from https://www.parentingteeens.about.com

U. S. Department of Health & Human Services (2008). Dealing with Risky Behaviors & Other Challenges. Illicit Drugs. Retrieved November 5, 2009 from www.4parents.gov

Warhiet, G. J., Vega, W. A., Khoury, E., Gil, A., & Elfenbein, P.H. (1996). A Comparative Analysis of Cigarette, Alcohol and Illicit Drug Use among an ethnically diverse sample of Hispanic, African Americans and Non-Hispanics. Journal of Drug Issues, 26, 901-922.

APPENDIX A
SURVEY

Appendix A: Questionnaire

Please read the following demographic questions and check the appropriate answer.

Please answer each question as you think your child would answer.

1. What is your child's age? Fill in the blank_____

2. What is your child's sex?

    a. Male

    b. Female

3. What is your ethnic background?

    a. White/European-American

    b. Black/African-American

    c. Asian/Pacific-Islander

    d. Hispanic/Latino

    e. Native American-Indian

    f. Other/multi-ethnic groups

4. What is your child's racial background?

    a. White/European-American

    b. Black/African-American

    c. Asian/Pacific-Islander

    d. Hispanic/Latino

    e. Native American-Indian

    f. Other/Multi-ethnic groups

5. What is your relationship to your child?

    a. Mother

    b. Father

    c. Other, (please specify) _____

6. Do you often talk with your child about substance use?

    a. Yes

    b. No

7. What grade is your child in?

    a. 7th

    b. 8th

    c. 9th

    d. 10th

    e. 11th

    f. 12th

8. Do you work full time?

    a. Yes

    b. No

9. Do you work part-time?

    a. Yes

    b. No

10. Do you work from home?

    a. Yes

    b. No

11. Do you work outside the home?

    a. Yes

    b. No

12. What income bracket do you consider yourself to be?

    a. Poor/lower class

    b. Working class

    c. Middle class

    d. Upper class

    e. Other (please specify)

13. Do you monitor your child's daily activities?

    a. Yes

    b. No

14. Have you had any experience with substance use?

    a. Yes

    b. No

15. Have you had experience with prevention programs?

    a. Yes

    b. No

16. Is there a drug/alcohol awareness program in your child's school?

    a. Yes

    b. No

    c. Don't know

The following questions pertain to Adolescents' Attitudes toward Substance Use. **Please answer each question as you think your child will answer.** If you think your child would do each of these things, mark y for yes. If you think your child would not do each of these things, mark N for no.

17. If your friends were doing something that would get them in trouble, would you try to stop them?

    a. Yes

    b. No

    c. Maybe

18. If one of your friends was smoking some marijuana and offered you some, would you smoke it?

   a. Yes

   b. No

   c. Maybe

The following is part two of Adolescents' Attitudes toward Substance Use. Please answer each question as you think your child would answer. Are the following statements mostly true or mostly false?

19. I will never drink beer, wine, or hard liquor.

   a. True

   b. False

20. I will never try marijuana or other drugs.

   a. True

   b. False

21. Smokers look stupid.

   a. True

   b. False

22. People my age who smoke are show-offs.

   a. True

   b. False

23. People who smoke marijuana have more fun than people who do not.

    a. True

    b. False

24. People my age smoke cigarettes have more friends than people who do not.

    a. True

    b. False

25. Smoking makes a person look grown up.

    a. True

    b. False

26. Girls like boys who smoke.

    a. True

    b. False

27. If a young person smokes marijuana, he or she will be popular.

    a. True

    b. False

The next series of questions pertain to Peer Drug Modeling. Please mark a. for "true" or b. for "false" for each of the following statements. **Please answer the questions as you think your child would answer.**

28. A friend has offered to share marijuana with me.

    a. True

    b. False

29. A friend has offered to share cigarettes with me.

    a. True

    b. False

30. I sometimes use marijuana or other drugs just because my friends are doing it.

    a. True

    b. False

The following questions pertain to Self-Esteem. Please tell whether you think each of the following statements are mostly true or mostly false about your child. **Please answer the questions as you think your child would answer.**

31. I am happy most of the time.

    a. True

    b. False

32. I am usually happy when I am at school.

    a. True

    b. False

33. Most of the time I am proud of myself.

    a. True

    b. False

34. Other students see me as a good student.

    a. True

    b. False

35. My grades at school are good.

    a. True

    b. False

36. I am proud of my school work.

    a. True

    b. False

37. Most boys and girls think I am good at school work.

    a. True

    b. False

38. I feel good about myself.

    a. True

    b. False

39. Sometimes I feel bad about myself.

    a. True

    b. False

40. Sometimes I think I am no good at all.

    a. True

    b. False

41. I often wish I were someone else.

    a. True

    b. False

42. I can't do anything well.

    a. True

    b. False

43. My teacher thinks that I am a slow learner.

    a. True

    b. False

44. Other boys and girls think I am a trouble maker.

    a. True

    b. False

The following statements pertains to your child's Positive Peer Modeling **Again, please answer the questions as you think your child would answer.** How important is it to you that your child's friends?

45. Are interested in the same things you are?

    a. Important

    b. Very Important

    c. Not important at all

46. Tell you the truth?

    a. Important

    b. Very Important

    c. Not important at all

47. Tell you how they feel?

    a. Important

    b. Very Important

    c. Not important at all

48. Help you with the problems they may have?

    a. Important

    b. Very Important

    c. Not important at all

49. Keep their promise?

    a. Important

    b. Very Important

    c. Not important at all

50. Care about you?

    a. Important

    b. Very Important

    c. Not important at all

Appendix D

Table 13

Descriptive Statistics for Perceptions of Attitudes towards Substance Use

Item	Yes N	Yes %	No N	No %	Maybe N	Maybe %
If your friends were doing something that would get them in trouble, would you try to stop them?	148	77.1	16	8.3	28	14.6
If one of your friends was smoking some marijuana and offered you some, would you smoke it?	6	3.1	151	77.4	38	19.5

Appendix E

Table 14
Descriptive Statistics for Perceptions of Attitudes towards Substance Use

	True N	True %	False N	False %
I will never drink beer, wine, or hard liquor.	127	65.1	68	34.9
I will never try marijuana or other drugs.	167	86.5	26	13.5
Smokers look stupid.	158	82.7	33	17.3
People my age who smoke are show-offs.	132	68.8	60	31.3
People who smoke marijuana have more fun than people who do not.	44	22.6	151	77.4
People my age who smoke cigarettes have more friends than people who do not.	36	18.5	159	81.5
Smoking makes a person look grown up.	29	15.0	164	85.0
Girls like boys who smoke.	12	6.3	180	93.8
If a person smokes marijuana, he or she will be popular.	16	8.2	178	91.8

Appendix F

Table 15

Descriptive Statistics for Perceptions of Peer Drug Modeling

	True		False	
Item	N	%	N	%
A friend has offered to share cigarettes with me.	104	54.2	88	45.8
A friend has offered to share marijuana with me.	46	24.3	143	75.7
I sometimes use marijuana or other drugs just because my friends are doing it.	12	6.3	180	93.8

Appendix G

Table 16
Descriptive Statistics for Perceptions of Self-Esteem

	True		False	
Item	N	%	N	%
I am happy most of the time.	179	94.2	11	5.8
I am usually happy when I am at school.	168	88.0	23	12.0
Most of the time I am proud of myself.	173	91.5	16	8.5
Other students see me as a good student.	173	91.5	16	8.5
My grades at school are good.	165	86.8	25	13.2
I am proud of my school work.	166	86.5	26	13.5
Most boys and girls think I am good at school work.	159	83.7	31	16.3
I feel good about myself.	172	90.5	18	9.5
Sometimes I feel bad about myself.	82	43.6	106	56.4
Sometimes I think I am no good at all.	33	17.3	158	82.7
I often wish I were someone else.	30	15.7	161	84.3
I can't do anything well.	13	6.8	179	93.2
My teacher thinks that I am a slow learner.	18	9.4	174	90.6
Other boys and girls think I am a trouble maker.	16	8.3	176	91.7

Appendix H

Table 17
Descriptive Statistics for Perceptions of Positive Peer Modeling

Item	Not Important at All N	%	Important N	%	Very Important N	%
Interested in same things they are	24	12.8	103	55.1	60	32.1
Telling the truth	5	2.8	79	43.6	97	53.6
Telling how they feel	17	9.4	112	62.2	51	28.3
Helping with problems they may have	12	6.7	116	64.8	51	28.5
Keeping their promise	2	1.1	86	48.3	90	50.6
Caring about them	2	1.1	108	60.0	70	38.9

Edwards Brothers Malloy
Thorofare, NJ USA
January 4, 2017